Popular Wine Regions

France

Grapes: Cabernet Sauvignon, Merlot, Cabernet Franc, Pinot Noir, Grenache, Syrah, Viognier, Chardonnay

Italy

Grapes: Sangiovese, Nebbiolo, Barbera, Moscato, Pinot Grigio

United States

Grapes: Cabernet Sauvignon, Pinot Noir, Chardonnay, Merlot, Zinfandel

Argentina

Grapes: Malbec, Bonarda

Chile

Grapes: Cabernet Sauvignon, Sauvignon Blanc

Australia

Grapes: Shiraz, Chardonnay

Germany

Grapes: Riesling, Gewurstraminer, Sylvaner

Spain

Grapes: Tempranillo, Albarino, Garnacha, Palomino

New Zealand

Grapes: Sauvignon Blanc, Pinot Noir

South Africa

Grapes: Pinotage, Chenin Blanc

Albariño	lemon, minerals
Breidecker	apple, pear
Chardonnay	butter, melon, apple, pineapple
Grüner Veltliner	green apple, citrus
Marsanne	almond, honeysuckle, marzipan
Melon de Bourgogne	lime, salt, green apple
Muscato	honey, grapes, lime
Pinot Grigio	buttery, smoky, earthy spice
Prosecco	apple, honey, musk, citrus
Riesling	citrus fruits, peach, honey
Sauvignon blanc	gooseberry, lime, asparagus
Sémillon	honey, orange, lime
Verdicchio	apple, minerals, citrus
Viognier	peach, pear, nutmeg, apricot

Red grape variety	Common sensory descriptors
Cabernet Franc	tobacco, green bell pepper
Cabernet Sauvignon	black currants, chocolate
Gamay	pomegranate, strawberry,
Grenache	smoky, pepper, raspberry
Merlot	black cherry, plums, tomato
Norton	red fruit, elderberries
Petite Sirah	earthy, black pepper, dark fruits
Petit Verdot	violets (later), pencil shavings
Pinot noir	raspberry, cherry, violets
Pinotage	bramble fruits
Sangiovese	herbs, black cherry, leathery
Syrah (Shiraz)	tobacco, black/white pepper
Tempranillo	vanilla, strawberry, tobacco
Teroldego	spices, chocolate, red fruits

Name of Wine _____

Region _____

Type _____ Vintage _____

Vineyard _____

Price _____ Date _____

Purchased/Received From _____

Serve With _____

Appearance _____

Bouquet _____

Taste _____

Body |—————————————————————————|
        Light   Medium   Full

Overall Rating

1   2   3   4   5   6   7   8   9   10

Additional Comments _____

_____

Attach Wine Label Here

Beauty is worse than wine; it intoxicates both the holder and the beholder." - Aldous

Name of Wine _____

Region _____

Type _____ Vintage _____

Vineyard _____

Price _____ Date _____

Purchased/Received From _____

Serve With _____

Appearance _____

Bouquet _____

Taste _____

Body |_____|
    Light   Medium   Full

Overall Rating

1 2 3 4 5 6 7 8 9 10

Additional Comments _____
_____

Attach Wine Label Here

"Beauty is worse than wine; it intoxicates both the holder and the beholder." - Aldous

Name of Wine _____

Region _____

Type _____ Vintage _____

Vineyard _____

Price _____ Date _____

Purchased/Received From _____

Serve With _____

Appearance _____

Bouquet _____

Taste _____

Body |_____|
    Light   Medium   Full

Overall Rating

1 2 3 4 5 6 7 8 9 10

Additional Comments _____

_____

"Beauty is worse than wine; it intoxicates both the holder and the beholder." - Aldous

Name of Wine _____

Region _____

Type _____ Vintage _____

Vineyard _____

Price _____ Date _____

Purchased/Received From _____

Serve With _____

Appearance _____

Bouquet _____

Taste _____

Body |_____|
     Light   Medium   Full

Overall Rating

1 2 3 4 5 6 7 8 9 10

Additional Comments _____
_____

Attach Wine Label Here

Name of Wine _____

Region _____

Type _____ Vintage _____

Vineyard _____

Price _____ Date _____

Purchased/Received From _____

Serve With _____

Appearance _____

Bouquet _____

Taste _____

Body |‾‾‾‾‾‾‾‾‾‾‾‾‾‾‾‾‾‾‾‾‾‾‾‾‾‾‾|
      Light   Medium   Full

Overall Rating

1 2 3 4 5 6 7 8 9 10

Additional Comments _____

_____

Attach Wine Label Here

"Beauty is worse than wine; it intoxicates both the holder and the beholder." - Aldous

Name of Wine _____

Region _____

Type _____ Vintage _____

Vineyard _____

Price _____ Date _____

Purchased/Received From _____

Serve With _____

Appearance _____

Bouquet _____

Taste _____

Body |_____|
      Light   Medium   Full

Overall Rating

1   2   3   4   5   6   7   8   9   10

Additional Comments _____

_____

"Beauty is worse than wine; it intoxicates both the holder and the beholder." - Aldous

Name of Wine _____

Region _____

Type _____ Vintage _____

Vineyard _____

Price _____ Date _____

Purchased/Received From _____

Serve With _____

Appearance _____

Bouquet _____

Taste _____

Body |_____|
    Light   Medium   Full

Overall Rating

1 2 3 4 5 6 7 8 9 10

Additional Comments _____

_____

Attach Wine Label Here

"Beauty is worse than wine; it intoxicates both the holder and the beholder." - Aldous

Name of Wine ....

Region ....

Type .... Vintage ....

Vineyard ....

Price .... Date ....

Purchased/Received From ....

Serve With ....

Appearance ....

Bouquet ....

Taste ....

Body |——————————————————|
    Light   Medium   Full

Overall Rating

1   2   3   4   5   6   7   8   9   10

Additional Comments ....

Attach Wine Label Here

"Beauty is worse than wine; it intoxicates both the holder and the beholder." - Aldous

Name of Wine _____

Region _____

Type _____ Vintage _____

Vineyard _____

Price _____ Date _____

Purchased/Received From _____

Serve With _____

Appearance _____

Bouquet _____

Taste _____

Body |_____|
    Light   Medium   Full

Overall Rating

1 2 3 4 5 6 7 8 9 10

Additional Comments _____

_____

Attach Wine Label Here

"Beauty is worse than wine; it intoxicates both the holder and the beholder." - Aldous

Name of Wine _____

Region _____

Type _____ Vintage _____

Vineyard _____

Price _____ Date _____

Purchased/Received From _____

Serve With _____

Appearance _____

Bouquet _____

Taste _____

Body | _____ |
    Light   Medium   Full

Overall Rating

1 2 3 4 5 6 7 8 9 10

Additional Comments _____

_____

Attach Wine Label Here

"Beauty is worse than wine; it intoxicates both the holder and the beholder." - Aldous

Name of Wine _____

Region _____

Type _____ Vintage _____

Vineyard _____

Price _____ Date _____

Purchased/Received From _____

Serve With _____

Appearance _____

Bouquet _____

Taste _____

Body |_____|
      Light   Medium   Full

Overall Rating

1   2   3   4   5   6   7   8   9   10

Additional Comments _____

_____

"Beauty is worse than wine; it intoxicates both the holder and the beholder." - Aldous

Name of Wine _____

Region _____

Type _____ Vintage _____

Vineyard _____

Price _____ Date _____

Purchased/Received From _____

Serve With _____

Appearance _____

Bouquet _____

Taste _____

Body |_____|
    Light   Medium   Full

Overall Rating

1 2 3 4 5 6 7 8 9 10

Additional Comments _____

_____

Attach Wine Label Here

"Beauty is worse than wine; it intoxicates both the holder and the beholder." - Aldous

Name of Wine _____

Region _____

Type _____ Vintage _____

Vineyard _____

Price _____ Date _____

Purchased/Received From _____

Serve With _____

Appearance _____

Bouquet _____

Taste _____

Body |‾‾‾‾‾‾‾‾‾‾‾‾‾‾‾‾‾‾‾‾‾‾‾‾|
     Light   Medium   Full

Overall Rating

1 2 3 4 5 6 7 8 9 10

Additional Comments _____

_____

Attach Wine Label Here

"Beauty is worse than wine; it intoxicates both the holder and the beholder." - Aldous

Name of Wine _____

Region _____

Type _____ Vintage _____

Vineyard _____

Price _____ Date _____

Purchased/Received From _____

Serve With _____

Appearance _____

Bouquet _____

Taste _____

Body |_____|
     Light   Medium   Full

Overall Rating

1   2   3   4   5   6   7   8   9   10

Additional Comments _____

_____

Attach Wine Label Here

"Beauty is worse than wine; it intoxicates both the holder and the beholder." - Aldous

Name of Wine _____

Region _____

Type _____ Vintage _____

Vineyard _____

Price _____ Date _____

Purchased/Received From _____

Serve With _____

Appearance _____

Bouquet _____

Taste _____

Body |_____|
     Light   Medium   Full

Overall Rating

1   2   3   4   5   6   7   8   9   10

Additional Comments _____

_____

"Beauty is worse than wine; it intoxicates both the holder and the beholder." - Aldous

Name of Wine _____

Region _____

Type _____ Vintage _____

Vineyard _____

Price _____ Date _____

Purchased/Received From _____

Serve With _____

Appearance _____

Bouquet _____

Taste _____

Body |_____|
     Light   Medium   Full

Overall Rating

1   2   3   4   5   6   7   8   9   10

Additional Comments _____
_____

Attach Wine Label Here

"Beauty is worse than wine; it intoxicates both the holder and the beholder." - Aldous

Name of Wine _____

Region _____

Type _____ Vintage _____

Vineyard _____

Price _____ Date _____

Purchased/Received From _____

Serve With _____

Appearance _____

Bouquet _____

Taste _____

Body |—————————————————————|
    Light   Medium   Full

Overall Rating

1   2   3   4   5   6   7   8   9   10

Additional Comments _____

_____

Attach Wine Label Here

"Beauty is worse than wine; it intoxicates both the holder and the beholder." - Aldous

Name of Wine _____

Region _____

Type _____ Vintage _____

Vineyard _____

Price _____ Date _____

Purchased/Received From _____

Serve With _____

Appearance _____

Bouquet _____

Taste _____

Body |_____|
    Light   Medium   Full

Overall Rating

1 2 3 4 5 6 7 8 9 10

Additional Comments _____

_____

Attach Wine Label Here

"Beauty is worse than wine; it intoxicates both the holder and the beholder." - Aldous

Name of Wine _____

Region _____

Type _____ Vintage _____

Vineyard _____

Price _____ Date _____

Purchased/Received From _____

Serve With _____

Appearance _____

Bouquet _____

Taste _____

Body |_____|
    Light   Medium   Full

Overall Rating

1 2 3 4 5 6 7 8 9 10

Additional Comments _____

_____

Attach Wine Label Here

"Beauty is worse than wine; it intoxicates both the holder and the beholder." - Aldous

Name of Wine _____

Region _____

Type _____ Vintage _____

Vineyard _____

Price _____ Date _____

Purchased/Received From _____

Serve With _____

Appearance _____

Bouquet _____

Taste _____

Body |——————————————————|
    Light   Medium   Full

Overall Rating

1 2 3 4 5 6 7 8 9 10

Additional Comments _____

_____

Attach Wine Label Here

"Beauty is worse than wine; it intoxicates both the holder and the beholder." - Aldous

Name of Wine _____

Region _____

Type _____ Vintage _____

Vineyard _____

Price _____ Date _____

Purchased/Received From _____

Serve With _____

Appearance _____

Bouquet _____

Taste _____

Body |—————————————————|
    Light   Medium   Full

Overall Rating

1 2 3 4 5 6 7 8 9 10

Additional Comments _____

_____

Attach Wine Label Here

"Beauty is worse than wine; it intoxicates both the holder and the beholder." - Aldous

Name of Wine _____

Region _____

Type _____ Vintage _____

Vineyard _____

Price _____ Date _____

Purchased/Received From _____

Serve With _____

Appearance _____

Bouquet _____

Taste _____

Body |_____|
     Light   Medium   Full

Overall Rating

1   2   3   4   5   6   7   8   9   10

Additional Comments _____

_____

Attach Wine Label Here

"Beauty is worse than wine; it intoxicates both the holder and the beholder." - Aldous

Name of Wine _____

Region _____

Type _____ Vintage _____

Vineyard _____

Price _____ Date _____

Purchased/Received From _____

Serve With _____

Appearance _____

Bouquet _____

Taste _____

Body |_____|
    Light   Medium   Full

Overall Rating

1 2 3 4 5 6 7 8 9 10

Additional Comments _____
_____

Attach Wine Label Here

"Beauty is worse than wine; it intoxicates both the holder and the beholder." - Aldous

Name of Wine _____

Region _____

Type _____ Vintage _____

Vineyard _____

Price _____ Date _____

Purchased/Received From _____

Serve With _____

Appearance _____

Bouquet _____

Taste _____

Body |_____|
    Light   Medium   Full

Overall Rating

1 2 3 4 5 6 7 8 9 10

Additional Comments _____

_____

Attach Wine Label Here

"Beauty is worse than wine; it intoxicates both the holder and the beholder." - Aldous

Name of Wine _____

Region _____

Type _____ Vintage _____

Vineyard _____

Price _____ Date _____

Purchased/Received From _____

Serve With _____

Appearance _____

Bouquet _____

Taste _____

Body |‾‾‾‾‾‾‾‾‾‾‾‾‾‾‾‾‾‾‾‾‾‾‾‾‾‾‾|
     Light   Medium   Full

Overall Rating

1   2   3   4   5   6   7   8   9   10

Additional Comments _____
_____

Attach Wine Label Here

"Beauty is worse than wine; it intoxicates both the holder and the beholder." - Aldous

Name of Wine _____

Region _____

Type _____ Vintage _____

Vineyard _____

Price _____ Date _____

Purchased/Received From _____

Serve With _____

Appearance _____

Bouquet _____

Taste _____

Body |_____|
    Light   Medium   Full

Overall Rating

1   2   3   4   5   6   7   8   9   10

Additional Comments _____

_____

"Beauty is worse than wine; it intoxicates both the holder and the beholder." - Aldous

Name of Wine _____

Region _____

Type _____ Vintage _____

Vineyard _____

Price _____ Date _____

Purchased/Received From _____

Serve With _____

Appearance _____

Bouquet _____

Taste _____

Body |_____|
    Light   Medium   Full

Overall Rating

1 2 3 4 5 6 7 8 9 10

Additional Comments _____

_____

Attach Wine Label Here

"Beauty is worse than wine; it intoxicates both the holder and the beholder." - Aldous

Name of Wine _____

Region _____

Type _____ Vintage _____

Vineyard _____

Price _____ Date _____

Purchased/Received From _____

Serve With _____

Appearance _____

Bouquet _____

Taste _____

Body |_____|
     Light   Medium   Full

Overall Rating

1   2   3   4   5   6   7   8   9   10

Additional Comments _____

_____

Attach Wine Label Here

Name of Wine _____

Region _____

Type _____ Vintage _____

Vineyard _____

Price _____ Date _____

Purchased/Received From _____

Serve With _____

Appearance _____

Bouquet _____

Taste _____

Body |‾‾‾‾‾‾‾‾‾‾‾‾‾‾‾‾‾‾‾‾‾‾‾‾‾|
     Light   Medium   Full

Overall Rating

1 2 3 4 5 6 7 8 9 10

Additional Comments _____

_____

Attach Wine Label Here

"Beauty is worse than wine; it intoxicates both the holder and the beholder." - Aldous

Name of Wine _____

Region _____

Type _____ Vintage _____

Vineyard _____

Price _____ Date _____

Purchased/Received From _____

Serve With _____

Appearance _____

Bouquet _____

Taste _____

Body |_____|
　　　Light　　　Medium　　　Full

Overall Rating

1　2　3　4　5　6　7　8　9　10

Additional Comments _____

_____

"Beauty is worse than wine; it intoxicates both the holder and the beholder." - Aldous

Name of Wine _____

Region _____

Type _____ Vintage _____

Vineyard _____

Price _____ Date _____

Purchased/Received From _____

Serve With _____

Appearance _____

Bouquet _____

Taste _____

Body |_____|
    Light   Medium   Full

Overall Rating

1 2 3 4 5 6 7 8 9 10

Additional Comments _____

_____

Attach Wine Label Here

"Beauty is worse than wine; it intoxicates both the holder and the beholder." - Aldous

Name of Wine _____

Region _____

Type _____ Vintage _____

Vineyard _____

Price _____ Date _____

Purchased/Received From _____

Serve With _____

Appearance _____

Bouquet _____

Taste _____

Body |_____|
     Light   Medium   Full

Overall Rating

1   2   3   4   5   6   7   8   9   10

Additional Comments _____

_____

Attach Wine Label Here

"Beauty is worse than wine; it intoxicates both the holder and the beholder." - Aldous

Name of Wine _____

Region _____

Type _____ Vintage _____

Vineyard _____

Price _____ Date _____

Purchased/Received From _____

Serve With _____

Appearance _____

Bouquet _____

Taste _____

Body |_____|
    Light   Medium   Full

Overall Rating

1   2   3   4   5   6   7   8   9   10

Additional Comments _____

_____

Attach Wine Label Here

Beauty is worse than wine; it intoxicates both the holder and the beholder." - Aldous

Name of Wine_____

Region _____

Type _____ Vintage _____

Vineyard _____

Price _____ Date _____

Purchased/Received From _____

Serve With _____

Appearance _____

Bouquet _____

Taste _____

Body |_____|
     Light   Medium   Full

Overall Rating

1   2   3   4   5   6   7   8   9   10

Additional Comments _____
_____

Attach Wine Label Here

"Beauty is worse than wine; it intoxicates both the holder and the beholder." - Aldous

Name of Wine ....

Region ....

Type .... Vintage ....

Vineyard ....

Price .... Date ....

Purchased/Received From ....

Serve With ....

Appearance ....

Bouquet ....

Taste ....

Body |‾‾‾‾‾‾‾‾‾‾‾‾‾‾‾‾‾‾‾‾‾‾‾‾‾‾‾‾‾‾‾‾‾|

     Light   Medium   Full

Overall Rating

1   2   3   4   5   6   7   8   9   10

Additional Comments ....

....

Attach Wine Label Here

"Beauty is worse than wine; it intoxicates both the holder and the beholder." - Aldous

Name of Wine _____

Region _____

Type _____ Vintage _____

Vineyard _____

Price _____ Date _____

Purchased/Received From _____

Serve With _____

Appearance _____

Bouquet _____

Taste _____

Body |_____|
    Light   Medium   Full

Overall Rating

1 2 3 4 5 6 7 8 9 10

Additional Comments _____
_____

Attach Wine Label Here

"Beauty is worse than wine; it intoxicates both the holder and the beholder." - Aldous

Name of Wine _____

Region _____

Type _____ Vintage _____

Vineyard _____

Price _____ Date _____

Purchased/Received From _____

Serve With _____

Appearance _____

Bouquet _____

Taste _____

Body |_____|
      Light   Medium   Full

Overall Rating

1   2   3   4   5   6   7   8   9   10

Additional Comments _____
_____

Attach Wine Label Here

"Beauty is worse than wine; it intoxicates both the holder and the beholder." - Aldous

Name of Wine _____

Region _____

Type _____ Vintage _____

Vineyard _____

Price _____ Date _____

Purchased/Received From _____

Serve With _____

Appearance _____

Bouquet _____

Taste _____

Body |_____|
    Light   Medium   Full

Overall Rating

1 2 3 4 5 6 7 8 9 10

Additional Comments _____

_____

Attach Wine Label Here

"Beauty is worse than wine; it intoxicates both the holder and the beholder." - Aldous

Name of Wine _____

Region _____

Type _____ Vintage _____

Vineyard _____

Price _____ Date _____

Purchased/Received From _____

Serve With _____

Appearance _____

Bouquet _____

Taste _____

Body |_____|
     Light   Medium   Full

Overall Rating

1 2 3 4 5 6 7 8 9 10

Additional Comments _____

_____

Attach Wine Label Here

"Beauty is worse than wine; it intoxicates both the holder and the beholder." - Aldous

Name of Wine ....

Region ....

Type .... Vintage ....

Vineyard ....

Price .... Date ....

Purchased/Received From ....

Serve With ....

Appearance ....

Bouquet ....

Taste ....

Body |_____|

　　Light　　　Medium　　　Full

Overall Rating

1　2　3　4　5　6　7　8　9　10

Additional Comments ....

....

Attach Wine Label Here

"Beauty is worse than wine; it intoxicates both the holder and the beholder." - Aldous

Name of Wine _____

Region _____

Type _____ Vintage _____

Vineyard _____

Price _____ Date _____

Purchased/Received From _____

Serve With _____

Appearance _____

Bouquet _____

Taste _____

Body |_____|
      Light   Medium   Full

Overall Rating

  1   2   3   4   5   6   7   8   9   10

Additional Comments _____

_____

Attach Wine Label Here

"Beauty is worse than wine; it intoxicates both the holder and the beholder." - Aldous

Name of Wine _____

Region _____

Type _____ Vintage _____

Vineyard _____

Price _____ Date _____

Purchased/Received From _____

Serve With _____

Appearance _____

Bouquet _____

Taste _____

Body |_____|
    Light   Medium   Full

Overall Rating

1 2 3 4 5 6 7 8 9 10

Additional Comments _____
_____

Attach Wine Label Here

"Beauty is worse than wine; it intoxicates both the holder and the beholder." - Aldous

Name of Wine _____

Region _____

Type _____ Vintage _____

Vineyard _____

Price _____ Date _____

Purchased/Received From _____

Serve With _____

Appearance _____

Bouquet _____

Taste _____

Body | _____ |
      Light   Medium   Full

Overall Rating

1 2 3 4 5 6 7 8 9 10

Additional Comments _____

_____

"Beauty is worse than wine; it intoxicates both the holder and the beholder." - Aldous

Name of Wine _____

Region _____

Type _____ Vintage _____

Vineyard _____

Price _____ Date _____

Purchased/Received From _____

Serve With _____

Appearance _____

Bouquet _____

Taste _____

Body |_____|
    Light   Medium   Full

Overall Rating

1 2 3 4 5 6 7 8 9 10

Additional Comments _____

_____

Attach Wine Label Here

"Beauty is worse than wine; it intoxicates both the holder and the beholder." - Aldous

Name of Wine _____

Region _____

Type _____ Vintage _____

Vineyard _____

Price _____ Date _____

Purchased/Received From _____

Serve With _____

Appearance _____

Bouquet _____

Taste _____

Body |‾‾‾‾‾‾‾‾‾‾‾‾‾‾‾‾‾‾‾‾‾‾‾‾‾|
     Light   Medium   Full

Overall Rating

1 2 3 4 5 6 7 8 9 10

Additional Comments _____

_____

Attach Wine Label Here

Beauty is worse than wine; it intoxicates both the holder and the beholder." - Aldous

Name of Wine _____

Region _____

Type _____ Vintage _____

Vineyard _____

Price _____ Date _____

Purchased/Received From _____

Serve With _____

Appearance _____

Bouquet _____

Taste _____

Body |_____|
     Light   Medium   Full

Overall Rating

1   2   3   4   5   6   7   8   9   10

Additional Comments _____

_____

Attach Wine Label Here

Name of Wine _____

Region _____

Type _____ Vintage _____

Vineyard _____

Price _____ Date _____

Purchased/Received From _____

Serve With _____

Appearance _____

Bouquet _____

Taste _____

Body |_____|
    Light   Medium   Full

Overall Rating

1 2 3 4 5 6 7 8 9 10

Additional Comments _____

_____

Attach Wine Label Here

"Beauty is worse than wine; it intoxicates both the holder and the beholder." - Aldous

Name of Wine _____

Region _____

Type _____ Vintage _____

Vineyard _____

Price _____ Date _____

Purchased/Received From _____

Serve With _____

Appearance _____

Bouquet _____

Taste _____

Body |_____|
       Light   Medium   Full

Overall Rating

1   2   3   4   5   6   7   8   9   10

Additional Comments _____

_____

Attach Wine Label Here

"Beauty is worse than wine; it intoxicates both the holder and the beholder." - Aldous

Name of Wine_____

Region_____

Type_____ Vintage_____

Vineyard_____

Price_____ Date_____

Purchased/Received From_____

Serve With_____

Appearance_____

Bouquet_____

Taste_____

Body |_____|
       Light   Medium   Full

Overall Rating

1   2   3   4   5   6   7   8   9   10

Additional Comments_____

_____

Attach Wine Label Here

"Beauty is worse than wine; it intoxicates both the holder and the beholder." - Aldous

Name of Wine _____

Region _____

Type _____ Vintage _____

Vineyard _____

Price _____ Date _____

Purchased/Received From _____

Serve With _____

Appearance _____

Bouquet _____

Taste _____

Body |‾‾‾‾‾‾‾‾‾‾‾‾‾‾‾‾‾‾‾‾‾‾‾‾‾|
     Light   Medium   Full

Overall Rating

1   2   3   4   5   6   7   8   9   10

Additional Comments _____

_____

Attach Wine Label Here

"Beauty is worse than wine; it intoxicates both the holder and the beholder." - Aldous

Name of Wine _____

Region _____

Type _____ Vintage _____

Vineyard _____

Price _____ Date _____

Purchased/Received From _____

Serve With _____

Appearance _____

Bouquet _____

Taste _____

Body |‾‾‾‾‾‾‾‾‾‾‾‾‾‾‾‾‾‾‾‾‾‾‾‾‾|
     Light   Medium   Full

Overall Rating

1   2   3   4   5   6   7   8   9   10

Additional Comments _____

_____

Name of Wine _____

Region _____

Type _____ Vintage _____

Vineyard _____

Price _____ Date _____

Purchased/Received From _____

Serve With _____

Appearance _____

Bouquet _____

Taste _____

Body |_____|
     Light   Medium   Full

Overall Rating

1   2   3   4   5   6   7   8   9   10

Additional Comments _____

_____

Attach Wine Label Here

"Beauty is worse than wine; it intoxicates both the holder and the beholder." - Aldous

Name of Wine _____

Region _____

Type _____ Vintage _____

Vineyard _____

Price _____ Date _____

Purchased/Received From _____

Serve With _____

Appearance _____

Bouquet _____

Taste _____

Body |_____|
　　　　Light　　　　　Medium　　　　　Full

Overall Rating

1　2　3　4　5　6　7　8　9　10

Additional Comments _____

_____

Attach Wine Label Here

"Beauty is worse than wine; it intoxicates both the holder and the beholder." - Aldous

Name of Wine _____

Region _____

Type _____ Vintage _____

Vineyard _____

Price _____ Date _____

Purchased/Received From _____

Serve With _____

Appearance _____

Bouquet _____

Taste _____

Body |—————————————————————|
     Light   Medium   Full

Overall Rating

1   2   3   4   5   6   7   8   9   10

Additional Comments _____

_____

Attach Wine Label Here

"Beauty is worse than wine; it intoxicates both the holder and the beholder." - Aldous

Name of Wine _____

Region _____

Type _____ Vintage _____

Vineyard _____

Price _____ Date _____

Purchased/Received From _____

Serve With _____

Appearance _____

Bouquet _____

Taste _____

Body |_____|
    Light   Medium   Full

Overall Rating

1 2 3 4 5 6 7 8 9 10

Additional Comments _____

_____

Attach Wine Label Here

"Beauty is worse than wine; it intoxicates both the holder and the beholder." - Aldous

Name of Wine _____

Region _____

Type _____ Vintage _____

Vineyard _____

Price _____ Date _____

Purchased/Received From _____

Serve With _____

Appearance _____

Bouquet _____

Taste _____

Body |———————————————————|
    Light   Medium   Full

Overall Rating

1 2 3 4 5 6 7 8 9 10

Additional Comments _____

_____

Attach Wine Label Here

"Beauty is worse than wine; it intoxicates both the holder and the beholder." - Aldous

Name of Wine ....

Region ....

Type .... Vintage ....

Vineyard ....

Price .... Date ....

Purchased/Received From ....

Serve With ....

Appearance ....

Bouquet ....

Taste ....

Body |_____|
       Light   Medium   Full

Overall Rating

  1   2   3   4   5   6   7   8   9   10

Additional Comments ....

....

Attach Wine Label Here

Beauty is worse than wine; it intoxicates both the holder and the beholder." - Aldous

Name of Wine _____

Region _____

Type _____ Vintage _____

Vineyard _____

Price _____ Date _____

Purchased/Received From _____

Serve With _____

Appearance _____

Bouquet _____

Taste _____

Body |_____|
      Light   Medium   Full

Overall Rating

1   2   3   4   5   6   7   8   9   10

Additional Comments _____

_____

Attach Wine Label Here

"Beauty is worse than wine; it intoxicates both the holder and the beholder." - Aldous

Name of Wine _____

Region _____

Type _____ Vintage _____

Vineyard _____

Price _____ Date _____

Purchased/Received From _____

Serve With _____

Appearance _____

Bouquet _____

Taste _____

Body |_____|
    Light   Medium   Full

Overall Rating

1 2 3 4 5 6 7 8 9 10

Additional Comments _____

_____

Attach Wine Label Here

"Beauty is worse than wine; it intoxicates both the holder and the beholder." - Aldous

Name of Wine _____

Region _____

Type _____ Vintage _____

Vineyard _____

Price _____ Date _____

Purchased/Received From _____

Serve With _____

Appearance _____

Bouquet _____

Taste _____

Body |‾‾‾‾‾‾‾‾‾‾‾‾‾‾‾‾‾‾‾‾‾‾‾‾‾‾‾|
     Light   Medium   Full

Overall Rating

1   2   3   4   5   6   7   8   9   10

Additional Comments _____

_____

Attach Wine Label Here

"Beauty is worse than wine; it intoxicates both the holder and the beholder." - Aldous

Name of Wine _____

Region _____

Type _____ Vintage _____

Vineyard _____

Price _____ Date _____

Purchased/Received From _____

Serve With _____

Appearance _____

Bouquet _____

Taste _____

Body |_____|
      Light   Medium   Full

Overall Rating

1 2 3 4 5 6 7 8 9 10

Additional Comments _____

_____

Attach Wine Label Here

"Beauty is worse than wine; it intoxicates both the holder and the beholder." - Aldous

Name of Wine _____

Region _____

Type _____ Vintage _____

Vineyard _____

Price _____ Date _____

Purchased/Received From _____

Serve With _____

Appearance _____

Bouquet _____

Taste _____

Body |_____|
     Light   Medium   Full

Overall Rating

1   2   3   4   5   6   7   8   9   10

Additional Comments _____

_____

Attach Wine Label Here

"Beauty is worse than wine; it intoxicates both the holder and the beholder." - Aldous

Name of Wine _____

Region _____

Type _____ Vintage _____

Vineyard _____

Price _____ Date _____

Purchased/Received From _____

Serve With _____

Appearance _____

Bouquet _____

Taste _____

Body |‾‾‾‾‾‾‾‾‾‾‾‾‾‾‾‾‾‾‾‾‾‾|
      Light   Medium   Full

Overall Rating

1 2 3 4 5 6 7 8 9 10

Additional Comments _____

_____

Attach Wine Label Here

"Beauty is worse than wine; it intoxicates both the holder and the beholder." - Aldous

Name of Wine _____

Region _____

Type _____ Vintage _____

Vineyard _____

Price _____ Date _____

Purchased/Received From _____

Serve With _____

Appearance _____

Bouquet _____

Taste _____

Body |_____|
     Light   Medium   Full

Overall Rating

1   2   3   4   5   6   7   8   9   10

Additional Comments _____

_____

Attach Wine Label Here

"Beauty is worse than wine; it intoxicates both the holder and the beholder." - Aldous

Name of Wine _____

Region _____

Type _____ Vintage _____

Vineyard _____

Price _____ Date _____

Purchased/Received From _____

Serve With _____

Appearance _____

Bouquet _____

Taste _____

Body |_____|
    Light   Medium   Full

Overall Rating

1   2   3   4   5   6   7   8   9   10

Additional Comments _____

_____

Attach Wine Label Here

"Beauty is worse than wine; it intoxicates both the holder and the beholder." - Aldous

Name of Wine _____

Region _____

Type _____ Vintage _____

Vineyard _____

Price _____ Date _____

Purchased/Received From _____

Serve With _____

Appearance _____

Bouquet _____

Taste _____

Body |_____|
     Light   Medium   Full

Overall Rating

1   2   3   4   5   6   7   8   9   10

Additional Comments _____

_____

Attach Wine Label Here

"Beauty is worse than wine; it intoxicates both the holder and the beholder." - Aldous

Name of Wine _____

Region _____

Type _____ Vintage _____

Vineyard _____

Price _____ Date _____

Purchased/Received From _____

Serve With _____

Appearance _____

Bouquet _____

Taste _____

Body |_____|
     Light   Medium   Full

Overall Rating

1 2 3 4 5 6 7 8 9 10

Additional Comments _____

_____

Attach Wine Label Here

"Beauty is worse than wine; it intoxicates both the holder and the beholder." - Aldous

Name of Wine..

Region..

Type.......................... Vintage..................

Vineyard..

Price.......................... Date..................

Purchased/Received From..

Serve With..

Appearance..

Bouquet..

Taste..

Body |_____|
　　　Light　　　　Medium　　　　Full

Overall Rating

1　2　3　4　5　6　7　8　9　10

Additional Comments..

....

Attach Wine Label Here

Name of Wine _____

Region _____

Type _____ Vintage _____

Vineyard _____

Price _____ Date _____

Purchased/Received From _____

Serve With _____

Appearance _____

Bouquet _____

Taste _____

Body |_____|
    Light   Medium   Full

Overall Rating

1 2 3 4 5 6 7 8 9 10

Additional Comments _____

_____

Attach Wine Label Here

"Beauty is worse than wine; it intoxicates both the holder and the beholder." - Aldous

Name of Wine _____

Region _____

Type _____ Vintage _____

Vineyard _____

Price _____ Date _____

Purchased/Received From _____

Serve With _____

Appearance _____

Bouquet _____

Taste _____

Body
| |
Light   Medium   Full

Overall Rating

1   2   3   4   5   6   7   8   9   10

Additional Comments _____

_____

Attach Wine Label Here

"Beauty is worse than wine; it intoxicates both the holder and the beholder." - Aldous

Name of Wine _____

Region _____

Type _____ Vintage _____

Vineyard _____

Price _____ Date _____

Purchased/Received From _____

Serve With _____

Appearance _____

Bouquet _____

Taste _____

Body |—————————————————|
      Light   Medium   Full

Overall Rating

1 2 3 4 5 6 7 8 9 10

Additional Comments _____
_____

Attach Wine Label Here

"Beauty is worse than wine; it intoxicates both the holder and the beholder." - Aldous

Name of Wine _____

Region _____

Type _____ Vintage _____

Vineyard _____

Price _____ Date _____

Purchased/Received From _____

Serve With _____

Appearance _____

Bouquet _____

Taste _____

Body |_____|
      Light   Medium   Full

Overall Rating

1   2   3   4   5   6   7   8   9   10

Additional Comments _____
_____

Attach Wine Label Here

"Beauty is worse than wine; it intoxicates both the holder and the beholder." - Aldous

Name of Wine _____

Region _____

Type _____ Vintage _____

Vineyard _____

Price _____ Date _____

Purchased/Received From _____

Serve With _____

Appearance _____

Bouquet _____

Taste _____

Body |_____|
     Light   Medium   Full

Overall Rating

1 2 3 4 5 6 7 8 9 10

Additional Comments _____
_____

Beauty is worse than wine; it intoxicates both the holder and the beholder." - Aldous

Name of Wine _____

Region _____

Type _____ Vintage _____

Vineyard _____

Price _____ Date _____

Purchased/Received From _____

Serve With _____

Appearance _____

Bouquet _____

Taste _____

Body |_____|
    Light   Medium   Full

Overall Rating

1 2 3 4 5 6 7 8 9 10

Additional Comments _____

_____

Attach Wine Label Here

"Beauty is worse than wine; it intoxicates both the holder and the beholder." - Aldous

Name of Wine _____

Region _____

Type _____ Vintage _____

Vineyard _____

Price _____ Date _____

Purchased/Received From _____

Serve With _____

Appearance _____

Bouquet _____

Taste _____

Body |_____|
    Light   Medium   Full

Overall Rating

1 2 3 4 5 6 7 8 9 10

Additional Comments _____

_____

Attach Wine Label Here

"Beauty is worse than wine; it intoxicates both the holder and the beholder." - Aldous

Name of Wine_____

Region_____

Type_____ Vintage_____

Vineyard_____

Price_____ Date_____

Purchased/Received From_____

Serve With_____

Appearance_____

Bouquet_____

Taste_____

Body |_____|
     Light   Medium   Full

Overall Rating

1   2   3   4   5   6   7   8   9   10

Additional Comments_____

_____

Attach Wine Label Here

"Beauty is worse than wine; it intoxicates both the holder and the beholder." - Aldous

Name of Wine _____

Region _____

Type _____ Vintage _____

Vineyard _____

Price _____ Date _____

Purchased/Received From _____

Serve With _____

Appearance _____

Bouquet _____

Taste _____

Body |_____|
    Light   Medium   Full

Overall Rating

1 2 3 4 5 6 7 8 9 10

Additional Comments _____

_____

Attach Wine Label Here

"Beauty is worse than wine; it intoxicates both the holder and the beholder." - Aldous

Name of Wine _____

Region _____

Type _____ Vintage _____

Vineyard _____

Price _____ Date _____

Purchased/Received From _____

Serve With _____

Appearance _____

Bouquet _____

Taste _____

Body |———————————————————|
       Light   Medium   Full

Overall Rating

1   2   3   4   5   6   7   8   9   10

Additional Comments _____
_____

Attach Wine Label Here

"Beauty is worse than wine; it intoxicates both the holder and the beholder." - Aldous

Name of Wine _____

Region _____

Type _____ Vintage _____

Vineyard _____

Price _____ Date _____

Purchased/Received From _____

Serve With _____

Appearance _____

Bouquet _____

Taste _____

Body |_____|
     Light   Medium   Full

Overall Rating

1 2 3 4 5 6 7 8 9 10

Additional Comments _____
_____

Attach Wine Label Here

"Beauty is worse than wine; it intoxicates both the holder and the beholder." - Aldous

Name of Wine _____

Region _____

Type _____ Vintage _____

Vineyard _____

Price _____ Date _____

Purchased/Received From _____

Serve With _____

Appearance _____

Bouquet _____

Taste _____

Body |_____|
    Light   Medium   Full

Overall Rating

1 2 3 4 5 6 7 8 9 10

Additional Comments _____
_____

Attach Wine Label Here

"Beauty is worse than wine; it intoxicates both the holder and the beholder." - Aldous

Name of Wine _____

Region _____

Type _____ Vintage _____

Vineyard _____

Price _____ Date _____

Purchased/Received From _____

Serve With _____

Appearance _____

Bouquet _____

Taste _____

Body |_____|
       Light   Medium   Full

Overall Rating

1   2   3   4   5   6   7   8   9   10

Additional Comments _____
_____

Attach Wine Label Here

Beauty is worse than wine; it intoxicates both the holder and the beholder." - Aldous

Name of Wine _____

Region _____

Type _____ Vintage _____

Vineyard _____

Price _____ Date _____

Purchased/Received From _____

Serve With _____

Appearance _____

Bouquet _____

Taste _____

Body |—————————————————————|
     Light   Medium   Full

Overall Rating

1   2   3   4   5   6   7   8   9   10

Additional Comments _____

_____

"Beauty is worse than wine; it intoxicates both the holder and the beholder." - Aldous

Name of Wine _____

Region _____

Type _____ Vintage _____

Vineyard _____

Price _____ Date _____

Purchased/Received From _____

Serve With _____

Appearance _____

Bouquet _____

Taste _____

Body |_____|
    Light   Medium   Full

Overall Rating

  1 2 3 4 5 6 7 8 9 10

Additional Comments _____

_____

Attach Wine Label Here

Beauty is worse than wine; it intoxicates both the holder and the beholder." - Aldous

Name of Wine _____

Region _____

Type _____ Vintage _____

Vineyard _____

Price _____ Date _____

Purchased/Received From _____

Serve With _____

Appearance _____

Bouquet _____

Taste _____

Body |_____|
      Light   Medium   Full

Overall Rating

1   2   3   4   5   6   7   8   9   10

Additional Comments _____

_____

"Beauty is worse than wine; it intoxicates both the holder and the beholder." - Aldous

Attach Wine Label Here

Name of Wine _____

Region _____

Type _____ Vintage _____

Vineyard _____

Price _____ Date _____

Purchased/Received From _____

Serve With _____

Appearance _____

Bouquet _____

Taste _____

Body |—————————————————|
    Light   Medium   Full

Overall Rating

1 2 3 4 5 6 7 8 9 10

Additional Comments _____

_____

Attach Wine Label Here

"Beauty is worse than wine; it intoxicates both the holder and the beholder." - Aldous

Name of Wine _____

Region _____

Type _____ Vintage _____

Vineyard _____

Price _____ Date _____

Purchased/Received From _____

Serve With _____

Appearance _____

Bouquet _____

Taste _____

Body |_____|
        Light   Medium   Full

Overall Rating

  1   2   3   4   5   6   7   8   9   10

Additional Comments _____
_____

Attach Wine Label Here

"Beauty is worse than wine; it intoxicates both the holder and the beholder." - Aldous

Name of Wine _____

Region _____

Type _____ Vintage _____

Vineyard _____

Price _____ Date _____

Purchased/Received From _____

Serve With _____

Appearance _____

Bouquet _____

Taste _____

Body |_____|
    Light   Medium   Full

Overall Rating

1 2 3 4 5 6 7 8 9 10

Additional Comments _____

_____

Attach Wine Label Here

"Beauty is worse than wine; it intoxicates both the holder and the beholder." - Aldous

Name of Wine _____

Region _____

Type _____ Vintage _____

Vineyard _____

Price _____ Date _____

Purchased/Received From _____

Serve With _____

Appearance _____

Bouquet _____

Taste _____

Body |_____|
     Light   Medium   Full

Overall Rating

1 2 3 4 5 6 7 8 9 10

Additional Comments _____

_____

Attach Wine Label Here

"Beauty is worse than wine; it intoxicates both the holder and the beholder." - Aldous

Name of Wine _____

Region _____

Type _____ Vintage _____

Vineyard _____

Price _____ Date _____

Purchased/Received From _____

Serve With _____

Appearance _____

Bouquet _____

Taste _____

Body |_____|
      Light   Medium   Full

Overall Rating

1   2   3   4   5   6   7   8   9   10

Additional Comments _____

_____

Attach Wine Label Here

"Beauty is worse than wine; it intoxicates both the holder and the beholder." - Aldous

Name of Wine _____

Region _____

Type _____ Vintage _____

Vineyard _____

Price _____ Date _____

Purchased/Received From _____

Serve With _____

Appearance _____

Bouquet _____

Taste _____

Body |—————————————————————|
     Light   Medium   Full

Overall Rating

1   2   3   4   5   6   7   8   9   10

Additional Comments _____

_____

Attach Wine Label Here

"Beauty is worse than wine; it intoxicates both the holder and the beholder." - Aldous

Name of Wine _____

Region _____

Type _____ Vintage _____

Vineyard _____

Price _____ Date _____

Purchased/Received From _____

Serve With _____

Appearance _____

Bouquet _____

Taste _____

Body |_____|
    Light   Medium   Full

Overall Rating

1 2 3 4 5 6 7 8 9 10

Additional Comments _____

_____

Attach Wine Label Here

"Beauty is worse than wine; it intoxicates both the holder and the beholder." - Aldous

Name of Wine _____

Region _____

Type _____ Vintage _____

Vineyard _____

Price _____ Date _____

Purchased/Received From _____

Serve With _____

Appearance _____

Bouquet _____

Taste _____

Body |_____|
   Light   Medium   Full

Overall Rating

1 2 3 4 5 6 7 8 9 10

Additional Comments _____

_____

Attach Wine Label Here

"Beauty is worse than wine; it intoxicates both the holder and the beholder." - Aldous

Name of Wine _____

Region _____

Type _____ Vintage _____

Vineyard _____

Price _____ Date _____

Purchased/Received From _____

Serve With _____

Appearance _____

Bouquet _____

Taste _____

Body |_____|
    Light   Medium   Full

Overall Rating

1 2 3 4 5 6 7 8 9 10

Additional Comments _____

_____

Attach Wine Label Here

"Beauty is worse than wine; it intoxicates both the holder and the beholder." - Aldous

Name of Wine _____

Region _____

Type _____ Vintage _____

Vineyard _____

Price _____ Date _____

Purchased/Received From _____

Serve With _____

Appearance _____

Bouquet _____

Taste _____

Body |—————————————|
    Light   Medium   Full

Overall Rating

1   2   3   4   5   6   7   8   9   10

Additional Comments _____

_____

Attach Wine Label Here

"Beauty is worse than wine; it intoxicates both the holder and the beholder." - Aldous

Name of Wine _____

Region _____

Type _____ Vintage _____

Vineyard _____

Price _____ Date _____

Purchased/Received From _____

Serve With _____

Appearance _____

Bouquet _____

Taste _____

Body |_____|
        Light   Medium   Full

Overall Rating

1   2   3   4   5   6   7   8   9   10

Additional Comments _____
_____

Attach Wine Label Here

"Beauty is worse than wine; it intoxicates both the holder and the beholder." - Aldous

Name of Wine _____

Region _____

Type _____ Vintage _____

Vineyard _____

Price _____ Date _____

Purchased/Received From _____

Serve With _____

Appearance _____

Bouquet _____

Taste _____

Body |_____|
    Light   Medium   Full

Overall Rating

  1   2   3   4   5   6   7   8   9   10

Additional Comments _____

_____

Attach Wine Label Here

"Beauty is worse than wine; it intoxicates both the holder and the beholder." - Aldous

Name of Wine ....

Region ....

Type .... Vintage ....

Vineyard ....

Price .... Date ....

Purchased/Received From ....

Serve With ....

Appearance ....

Bouquet ....

Taste ....

Body |_____|
　　　Light　　　　Medium　　　　Full

Overall Rating

1　2　3　4　5　6　7　8　9　10

Additional Comments ....

Attach Wine Label Here

"Beauty is worse than wine; it intoxicates both the holder and the beholder." - Aldous

Name of Wine _____

Region _____

Type _____ Vintage _____

Vineyard _____

Price _____ Date _____

Purchased/Received From _____

Serve With _____

Appearance _____

Bouquet _____

Taste _____

Body |_____|
      Light   Medium   Full

Overall Rating

  1   2   3   4   5   6   7   8   9   10

Additional Comments _____

_____

Attach Wine Label Here

"Beauty is worse than wine; it intoxicates both the holder and the beholder." - Aldous

Name of Wine ....

Region ....

Type .... Vintage ....

Vineyard ....

Price .... Date ....

Purchased/Received From ....

Serve With ....

Appearance ....

Bouquet ....

Taste ....

Body |————————————————————|
    Light   Medium   Full

Overall Rating

1 2 3 4 5 6 7 8 9 10

Additional Comments ....

....

Attach Wine Label Here

"Beauty is worse than wine; it intoxicates both the holder and the beholder." - Aldous

Name of Wine ....

Region ....

Type .... Vintage ....

Vineyard ....

Price .... Date ....

Purchased/Received From ....

Serve With ....

Appearance ....

Bouquet ....

Taste ....

Body |_____|
    Light   Medium   Full

Overall Rating

  1 2 3 4 5 6 7 8 9 10

Additional Comments ....
....

Attach Wine Label Here

"Beauty is worse than wine; it intoxicates both the holder and the beholder." - Aldous

Name of Wine _____

Region _____

Type _____ Vintage _____

Vineyard _____

Price _____ Date _____

Purchased/Received From _____

Serve With _____

Appearance _____

Bouquet _____

Taste _____

Body |‾‾‾‾‾‾‾‾‾‾‾‾‾‾‾‾‾‾‾‾‾‾‾‾|
    Light   Medium   Full

Overall Rating

1 2 3 4 5 6 7 8 9 10

Additional Comments _____
_____

Attach Wine Label Here

"Beauty is worse than wine; it intoxicates both the holder and the beholder." - Aldous

Name of Wine _____

Region _____

Type _____ Vintage _____

Vineyard _____

Price _____ Date _____

Purchased/Received From _____

Serve With _____

Appearance _____

Bouquet _____

Taste _____

Body |——————————————|
      Light   Medium   Full

Overall Rating

1   2   3   4   5   6   7   8   9   10

Additional Comments _____

_____

Attach Wine Label Here

"Beauty is worse than wine; it intoxicates both the holder and the beholder." - Aldous

Name of Wine _____

Region _____

Type _____ Vintage _____

Vineyard _____

Price _____ Date _____

Purchased/Received From _____

Serve With _____

Appearance _____

Bouquet _____

Taste _____

Body |‾‾‾‾‾‾‾‾‾‾‾‾‾‾‾‾‾‾‾‾‾‾‾‾‾|
    Light   Medium   Full

Overall Rating

1 2 3 4 5 6 7 8 9 10

Additional Comments _____

_____

Attach Wine Label Here

"Beauty is worse than wine; it intoxicates both the holder and the beholder." - Aldous

Name of Wine _____

Region _____

Type _____ Vintage _____

Vineyard _____

Price _____ Date _____

Purchased/Received From _____

Serve With _____

Appearance _____

Bouquet _____

Taste _____

Body |_____|
     Light   Medium   Full

Overall Rating

  1   2   3   4   5   6   7   8   9   10

Additional Comments _____
_____

Attach Wine Label Here

"Beauty is worse than wine; it intoxicates both the holder and the beholder." - Aldous

Name of Wine _____

Region _____

Type _____ Vintage _____

Vineyard _____

Price _____ Date _____

Purchased/Received From _____

Serve With _____

Appearance _____

Bouquet _____

Taste _____

Body |_____|
    Light   Medium   Full

Overall Rating

1   2   3   4   5   6   7   8   9   10

Additional Comments _____

_____

Attach Wine Label Here

"Beauty is worse than wine; it intoxicates both the holder and the beholder." - Aldous

Name of Wine _____

Region _____

Type _____ Vintage _____

Vineyard _____

Price _____ Date _____

Purchased/Received From _____

Serve With _____

Appearance _____

Bouquet _____

Taste _____

Body |_____|
    Light   Medium   Full

Overall Rating

1 2 3 4 5 6 7 8 9 10

Additional Comments _____

_____

Attach Wine Label Here

"Beauty is worse than wine; it intoxicates both the holder and the beholder." - Aldous

Name of Wine _____

Region _____

Type _____ Vintage _____

Vineyard _____

Price _____ Date _____

Purchased/Received From _____

Serve With _____

Appearance _____

Bouquet _____

Taste _____

Body |_____|
     Light   Medium   Full

Overall Rating

1   2   3   4   5   6   7   8   9   10

Additional Comments _____

_____

"Beauty is worse than wine; it intoxicates both the holder and the beholder." - Aldous

Name of Wine _____

Region _____

Type _____ Vintage _____

Vineyard _____

Price _____ Date _____

Purchased/Received From _____

Serve With _____

Appearance _____

Bouquet _____

Taste _____

Body | _____ |
    Light   Medium   Full

Overall Rating

1 2 3 4 5 6 7 8 9 10

Additional Comments _____

_____

Attach Wine Label Here

"Beauty is worse than wine; it intoxicates both the holder and the beholder." - Aldous

Name of Wine _____

Region _____

Type _____ Vintage _____

Vineyard _____

Price_____ Date _____

Purchased/Received From _____

Serve With _____

Appearance _____

Bouquet _____

Taste _____

Body |_____|
    Light   Medium   Full

Overall Rating

1 2 3 4 5 6 7 8 9 10

Additional Comments _____
_____

"Beauty is worse than wine; it intoxicates both the holder and the beholder." - Aldous

Name of Wine _____

Region _____

Type _____ Vintage _____

Vineyard _____

Price _____ Date _____

Purchased/Received From _____

Serve With _____

Appearance _____

Bouquet _____

Taste _____

Body |⎿_____⏋|
    Light   Medium   Full

Overall Rating

1 2 3 4 5 6 7 8 9 10

Additional Comments _____

_____

Attach Wine Label Here

"Beauty is worse than wine; it intoxicates both the holder and the beholder." - Aldous

Name of Wine _____

Region _____

Type _____ Vintage _____

Vineyard _____

Price _____ Date _____

Purchased/Received From _____

Serve With _____

Appearance _____

Bouquet _____

Taste _____

Body |⎵⎵⎵⎵⎵⎵⎵⎵⎵⎵⎵⎵⎵⎵⎵|
     Light   Medium   Full

Overall Rating

1   2   3   4   5   6   7   8   9   10

Additional Comments _____

_____

Attach Wine Label Here

"Beauty is worse than wine; it intoxicates both the holder and the beholder." - Aldous

Name of Wine _____

Region _____

Type _____ Vintage _____

Vineyard _____

Price _____ Date _____

Purchased/Received From _____

Serve With _____

Appearance _____

Bouquet _____

Taste _____

Body |_____|
      Light   Medium   Full

Overall Rating

1   2   3   4   5   6   7   8   9   10

Additional Comments _____
_____

Attach Wine Label Here

"Beauty is worse than wine; it intoxicates both the holder and the beholder." - Aldous

Name of Wine _____

Region _____

Type _____ Vintage _____

Vineyard _____

Price _____ Date _____

Purchased/Received From _____

Serve With _____

Appearance _____

Bouquet _____

Taste _____

Body |_____|
        Light   Medium   Full

Overall Rating

  1   2   3   4   5   6   7   8   9   10

Additional Comments _____

_____

Attach Wine Label Here

Name of Wine _____

Region _____

Type _____ Vintage _____

Vineyard _____

Price _____ Date _____

Purchased/Received From _____

Serve With _____

Appearance _____

Bouquet _____

Taste _____

Body |_____|
     Light   Medium   Full

Overall Rating

1   2   3   4   5   6   7   8   9   10

Additional Comments _____

_____

Attach Wine Label Here

"Beauty is worse than wine; it intoxicates both the holder and the beholder." - Aldous

Name of Wine _____

Region _____

Type _____ Vintage _____

Vineyard _____

Price _____ Date _____

Purchased/Received From _____

Serve With _____

Appearance _____

Bouquet _____

Taste _____

Body |_____|
    Light   Medium   Full

Overall Rating

1 2 3 4 5 6 7 8 9 10

Additional Comments _____

Attach Wine Label Here

"Beauty is worse than wine; it intoxicates both the holder and the beholder." - Aldous

Name of Wine _____

Region _____

Type _____ Vintage _____

Vineyard _____

Price _____ Date _____

Purchased/Received From _____

Serve With _____

Appearance _____

Bouquet _____

Taste _____

Body |⎯⎯⎯⎯⎯⎯⎯⎯⎯⎯⎯⎯⎯|
       Light   Medium   Full

Overall Rating

  1   2   3   4   5   6   7   8   9   10

Additional Comments _____
_____

Attach Wine Label Here

"Beauty is worse than wine; it intoxicates both the holder and the beholder." - Aldous

Name of Wine _____

Region _____

Type _____ Vintage _____

Vineyard _____

Price _____ Date _____

Purchased/Received From _____

Serve With _____

Appearance _____

Bouquet _____

Taste _____

Body |_____|
        Light   Medium   Full

Overall Rating

    1   2   3   4   5   6   7   8   9   10

Additional Comments _____

_____

Attach Wine Label Here

"Beauty is worse than wine; it intoxicates both the holder and the beholder." - Aldous

Name of Wine _____

Region _____

Type _____ Vintage _____

Vineyard _____

Price _____ Date _____

Purchased/Received From _____

Serve With _____

Appearance _____

Bouquet _____

Taste _____

Body |_____|
    Light   Medium   Full

Overall Rating

1 2 3 4 5 6 7 8 9 10

Additional Comments _____

Attach Wine Label Here

"Beauty is worse than wine; it intoxicates both the holder and the beholder." - Aldous

Name of Wine _____

Region _____

Type _____ Vintage _____

Vineyard _____

Price _____ Date _____

Purchased/Received From _____

Serve With _____

Appearance _____

Bouquet _____

Taste _____

Body |‾‾‾‾‾‾‾‾‾‾‾‾‾‾‾‾‾‾‾‾‾‾‾‾‾‾‾|
    Light   Medium   Full

Overall Rating

  1 2 3 4 5 6 7 8 9 10

Additional Comments _____

_____

Attach Wine Label Here

Beauty is worse than wine; it intoxicates both the holder and the beholder." - Aldous